MW00876524

Montessori at Home Guide

A SHORT INTRODUCTION TO MARIA
MONTESSORI AND A PRACTICAL GUIDE
TO APPLY HER INSPIRATION AT HOME
FOR CHILDREN AGES 0-2

A. M. Sterling

Illustrations by: Robert McKinney

Sterling Production
LEXINGTON, KENTUCKY

Sterling Production
www.sterlingproduction.com
ashleyandmitch@sterlingproduction.com

Montessori at Home Guide: A Short Introduction to Maria Montessori and a Practical Guide to Apply her Inspiration at Home for Children Ages 0-2 / A. M. Sterling —2nd ed.
ISBN-13: 978-1540677754
ISBN-10: 1540677753

Contents

Dedicated to our son Mars.

"The goal of early childhood education should be to activate the child's own natural desire to learn."

-MARIA MONTESSORI

CHAPTER ONE

Introduction

Becoming a parent is a life changing experience. From day one, you experience feelings and emotions that words cannot quite describe. The importance of your baby's new life seems to make everything else pale in comparison.

During this special time, it's natural for new and even seasoned parents to have questions about how to best parent their children. If you're reading this book, you've probably begun searching for some answers surrounding parenthood and how to care for your little one. This guide has been created to help answer your questions and provide some direction for how to incorporate the Montessori philosophy into your parenting from day one.

Throughout this book, you will also find excerpts from an interview conducted with Anastasia of www.montessorinature.com. On her website, she shares fantastic ways to incorporate the ideas of Maria Montessori into raising compassionate, independent, happy and successful children. Montessori Nature Blog is dedicated to sharing fun, nature-centered, meaningful learning experiences, DIY activities and tips. It includes printable educational materials as well as online resources which are wonderful time-savers for teachers and parents alike. We consider Anastasia, not only a friend, but one of most knowledgeable Montessori experts among our younger generation.

From birth to age 2, your baby will grow and change immensely. While just about any stranger will tell you that babies grow up so fast, there's nothing quite like experiencing it first-hand. Each of the special "firsts" your baby reaches will amaze you as you marvel at how quickly your little one is growing and changing. In this guide, we'll also include some of the milestones you can celebrate with your child and when to expect them. This will help you gauge your child's progress and prepare for the next steps.

Each stage brings its own joys and struggles. You'll find that just as soon as your child finishes one phase, another will begin. Whether it's a crying, colic schedule or finding great joy in dropping toys, each phase represents a stage of your child's development.

"[The] Life of Maria Montessori is a combination of untamed passion, determination and extremely hard work. There is one particular fact from her life that pushed me to become her faithful follower. During her medical study, she reached a point of wanting to abandon her study due to great hardships she faced being a female medical student. At that time, she had an encounter that, I believe, determined the rest of her destiny. On the street Maria saw a destitute child who was totally absorbed playing with a piece of red paper. She was fascinated by the way that poor child was able to focus. She recognized the great potential that lay within every human being. That encouraged her to complete the study and open her first school for children with severe learning difficulties who lived in an asylum for mentally disabled children. She had astounding success. "It is necessary to place human dignity within their grasp", she said. This remarkable passion to release child's potential fascinates me the most."

-ANASTASIA

Montessori's observations and research in childhood development provide some excellent resources for better understanding our children and their intellectual, emotional and physical growth. Beginning her career as a doctor in the late 1800s, Montessori took an interest to psychology. She first worked with children who were considered mentally ill, developing many of her materials and classroom guidelines in the process. Her extensive time spent with families and children, observing their development, led to the creation of a philosophy that now guides thousands of parents, teachers and children around the world.

During the years from 0-2, Montessori believed that the main need of the child is to be connected with, loved by and to build trust with her parents, particularly with the mother. A second, conflicting, but equally important need is independence. These two themes are played out in a young child's life, as they cry for comfort, attention and nourishment, but also make great efforts to build the necessary muscle and neural connections to sit, crawl and stand on their own.

These needs, along with other helpful insights from Montessori and more modern early childhood specialists in combination with the helpful techniques and activities provided in this guide will help you along your parenting journey. The greater we understanding our children's development and journey, the better we can guide them in their growth.

As you begin your parenting journey for the first time, or experience a fresh start with a new child, remember that ultimately, your parenting decisions are yours and yours alone. At times, it may feel like advice comes in from all sides, and you may be unsure of what to do. However, as every parent does, you'll find your own path and develop your own unique parenting style that fits you and your child.

We wish you the best as you embark on this amazing journey!

"The baby's fundamental need – precisely because he is a human being – is to be loved. But it takes a mature person to love a baby, because love takes time, love takes patience, love takes fortitude, love even requires a certain kind of humility: to love another better than one's self. The baby needs time to be understood: he needs time in everything he does."

-MARIA MONTESSORI

CHAPTER TWO

0-6 Months

Birth and the first six months of life are marked by the great change from living in the womb to living in the outside world. During the first few months of life, your baby will sleep a lot, enjoy being held, sung to and talked to. In this stage, your baby will enjoy your presence more than anything else. You may feel that all your baby does for the first while is eat, sleep, poop and cry. However, as Montessori so aptly put it in her book *The Absorbent Mind*, "Man seems to have two embryonic periods. One is prenatal…the other is postnatal." Babies are born largely helpless and completely dependent on their parents for care. This is because brain development could not possibly continue in the womb, as the size of the head would be too large for birth.

In the first months of life, a great deal of basic development continues to happen in your child. Brain development is of particular importance. You'll also observe as your child quickly outgrows their clothes, leaving newborn sized outfits behind in a matter of weeks. Within the first year of life, babies often more than double their weight. This time is full of advances and growth as your newborn begins forming their character and learns to become a person. Let's take a look at some of the milestones to be expected during the first 6 months of life.

Milestones

Milestones are helpful markers that can indicate to parents when most children show a certain behavior. However, keep in mind that each child develops at her own rate. While milestones are helpful for letting you know what to expect, don't worry if your child varies from these typical patterns. If you have concerns about your child's development, speak with your child's pediatrician.

Take a look at what you can expect during your baby's first 6 months of life:

- **1 month old**
    - Your baby's eyesight is still developing. About 8-12 inches away is the farthest away she can focus.
    - Your baby may be able to lift their head for a short time when lying on their stomach.
    - Your baby has likely become an expert sucker, whether they're breastfed or bottle fed, they know what to do.
- **3 months old**
    - Your baby may smile and/or laugh by around this time.
    - Your baby may start making cooing noises.
    - Your baby is stronger and able to hold their head up well.

- ○ Your baby has developed quite the grasp and may be able to hold on to toys and shake them.
- **6 months old**
    - ○ Your baby is ready for solid food! If you haven't already begun, now is a great time to start.
    - ○ Your baby can roll over by now, and may even have quite a bit of practice.
    - ○ Your baby is either sitting up on their own or getting very close to doing so!
    - ○ Your baby probably enjoys reaching and grabbing at objects and interacts more during play.

Now that you have some idea of what to expect during this time period, we'll move on to discuss some of the fun ways that you can interact with your baby to encourage their growth and development.

Materials

Montessori first and foremost advocated for infants to be included in daily life. While they can do little to participate, infants are taking in everything around them. Sounds, smells, sights, touch and movements are all absorbed by the infant. This is how they learn and develop.

In order to stimulate infants and help them in their development, Montessori developed a number of helpful materials and suggestions for parents and educators to use. Some great items to prepare or purchase include mobiles, books and mirrors.

Because infants begin learning with their senses, these items are excellent options to start with as they are visually stimulating.

A note about making and purchasing materials:

Montessori advocated using items made of natural materials such as wood, metal, cloth and other natural fibers. Flashy plastic toys with buttons and lights can often overstimulate the child and take away from the child's ability to concentrate and interact with the material. When colors are used in materials, they often serve a specific purpose such as for color matching, assisting in memorizing shapes (such as the continents), or as a theme. Materials are meant to be used in a certain way. So, as you advance and use more challenging materials with your child, encourage them to use the materials in the correct way.

Mobiles

Montessori mobiles can be purchased or made. Traditionally, the first mobiles introduced to a baby feature the colors black and white. As discussed in the milestones, a young baby's eyesight is not very good. For this reason, the contrasts between black and white are easy for them to see and are quite appealing. Keep in mind, that mobiles should be placed 8 to 12 inches from the child's face.

Then, mobiles including colors may be used. First the primary colors are featured. Then, another popular Montessori mobile is designed to display shades of one color on a mobile. For instance, a range of shades from a deep red to a very light pink may be featured. Beginning with primary colors, these shaded mobiles may be used, moving on to secondary colors.

Touchable or tactile mobiles may be introduced when the baby becomes interested in touching and grabbing. These mobiles often feature a bell. This way, the sense of hearing is also involved in play.

Books

Even young babies of a few months of age can enjoy looking at books. Sturdy, cardboard books are the best options. For this age, Montessori recommended using only real images. Because young children are still grasping reality, she believed it was best to focus on grounding them in the real world before sharing fantastical books with them. There are many baby books available that feature wonderful photos of real objects, people and animals.

Mirrors

Try hanging a mirror at a very low level in a space where your baby spends a lot of time. Above a thick rug or blanketed area on the floor will ensure she will be comfortable. You will find that your little one will enjoy looking at themselves.

These are materials you can enjoy with your baby, or that he or she can enjoy on their own. You can lie down with your baby to look at the mobile and gently move it for them. Or, spend time reading a book together. Practice making funny faces in the mirror together.

You can try sticking out your tongue or touching your face to see if your baby copies you.

Cloth Diapers

While these aren't really a material for your baby to interact with, potty learning begins from birth. Cloth diapers are the first step in potty learning, although this stage of potty learning isn't as intense as later on. Cloth diapers are preferable as your child will be more able to sense the wetness that occurs after urinating. Sensitivity to this sensation is how children become more aware of their body's processes as they grow. Consider using cloth diapers if at all possible to help improve the potty learning process later on.

Enjoying Time with Your Baby

As mentioned, Montessori advocated for babies to be included in daily life. For this reason, consider using a baby carrier or similar option so that you can take your baby anywhere you go, easily. Your baby will gain much from participating in your daily activities, attached to you! For example, when shopping, they'll see all of the people and the store or market where you shop. Or, they'll see running water as you do the dishes. When cooking, your baby will smell the delicious smells and hear you chopping.

A few other helpful and important activities to enjoy with your newborn are singing and talking. Although at first, it may feel like you're talking to a wall, with time, you'll find it natural to talk to your baby. Try telling your baby about what you're doing. Or, count their toes and sing a song when changing their diaper.

Many parents also enjoy listening to music and dancing with their little ones. This is a great way to stimulate the senses and gives your baby the chance to hear music and feel movement.

The Perfect Environment

Montessori called the first few years of life the years of the absorbent mind. Infants and young children must absorb everything in their surroundings in order to learn. This is a process that happens naturally. For this reason, Montessori called it "unconscious creation." During this time, children, out of pure absorption, learn to talk, walk, and control movements, leading to independence. This special time of the absorbent mind from birth to about 3 years of age should be taken advantage of. Part of the way you can do this is through creating a wonderful environment for your child.

"Children absorb and become everything they feel, see, touch, smell, and hear from birth. As a parent, I have responsibility to ensure that environment surrounding my child is safe, stress free, filled with love and care. Hence, I aim to create atmosphere of peace and acceptance by establishing loving relationships with everyone in the house. This is the most essential aspect I would like my children to absorb from the start, and know that they are safe to learn, play, make mistakes and give love in return. Secondary, I provide opportunities to discover and learn by setting up an environment that is pleasant, uncluttered, filled with age appropriate challenges and contains wide range of sensory stimulations. Babies love resting underneath trees, watch leaves and branches move in the wind. Beach outings are our favorite! My baby enjoys feeling sand running between his fingers and tickling his toes. When taking a bath, I add a couple drops of pure lavender oil for pleasant smell that is perfect to calm baby before night rest."

-ANASTASIA

Montessori suggested that parents create a safe space for their baby, including a bed on the floor, rather than a crib. She advocated for freedom of movement, rather than strapping babies into chairs, enclosing them in cribs and keeping them largely immobile. With a floor bed, the baby learns quickly how to get in and out of the bed safely. While for the first month or two, many parents use a Moses basket, bassinet, or practice co-sleeping, after this stage, they can be transferred to a floor bed. The floor bed should stay located in the parents' bedroom at least until the six-month mark to reduce the chances of SIDS.

Aside from the bed on the floor, many parents following Montessori principles choose to include a few low shelves containing baby-safe objects such as books and toys made from natural materials. Some of these toys may include wooden puzzles (with large pieces) or items made of cloth. Low hanging pictures are also great to include.

Child-sized furniture is also encouraged, so that as the baby grows, they can make use of it. Of course, you can prepare your baby's room and make adjustments as they grow and develop, introducing furniture when it is appropriate.

Ensure that your baby's nursery is organized and clean. Even from a young age, Montessori believed that young children appreciate order, and are actually very interested in this from birth through about age 5. In addition to an orderly environment, these young children appreciate routines and predictable schedules. As children grow, the sensitivity to physical order gives way to a need for mental order – explaining the typical teenage pattern of messiness. Yet, for our babies, order is essential. It's soothing and helps meet their need of consistency and repetition.

You and Your Baby from 0-6 Months

During these first six months, you'll learn to understand your child. You'll be able to predict when they're hungry and sleepy. You'll know what some of their favorite activities and objects are.

Treasure these special times that you enjoy with your young baby. Although there are difficult moments of sleeplessness, colic and some who experience trouble feeding, the joys overcome these trials. You and your baby will be so close by the end of the first six months, you may feel as though you are not separate beings.

Yet, slowly but surely, your baby will begin to develop independence and grow to be her very own person. From 0-6 months, you'll begin the relationship with this wonderful being who will always be a part of your life.

"Follow the child, they will show you what they need to do, what they need to develop in themselves and what area they need to be challenged in. "

-MARIA MONTESSORI

CHAPTER THREE

6-12 Months

From 6-12 months, your baby will continue to grow at a rapid rate. There are many exciting and interesting adventures during this stage. Eating solids is certainly one of the highlights and watching your child try all sorts of new food is very exciting.

Another important theme during this stage is independence. Your baby is likely sitting by now, or will be soon! Many babies begin to crawl and are even walking by the time they reach one-year-old. However, trust your child to move at their own pace. Should you have any concerns, it's always best to consult with your child's pediatrician to be sure that there's no cause for concern.

Additionally, your baby will probably become much more attached to you and may experience anxiety when strangers or unfamiliar people interact with them. This is normal and natural as your baby becomes ever more aware of their surroundings.

This is a fun age of discovery as your child also improves on their fine and gross motor skills. Play is more interactive. Your baby now recognizes when you say their name and may babble back at you. During this exciting time, there are many more activities and experiences that you will be able to share with your baby. As you continue to watch your baby grow, they will continue to achieve new milestones with incredible speed.

Milestones

Always remember that each child develops at their own pace. As tempting as it may be to compare your baby's achievements to nieces, nephews and other little ones, remember that each baby is unique. Some are quick to talk, while others sit up and crawl early. Yet others take their time to reach milestones, but are doing just fine. Should you feel concerned about your baby's progress, consult with a professional.

- **7 months old**
  - Your baby can probably sit up on their own now.
  - Your baby may be showing signs of crawling. There are many styles of crawling! Some only go backwards, some roll and others scoot.
  - Teething. Your baby may teeth for a month or more before you even see a tooth emerging from their gums.
  - Even if your baby doesn't have teeth yet, their gums are good for mashing. Try feeding your baby mashed up cooked vegetables and fruits.

- **9 months old**

- By now your baby can probably stand while holding onto something for support and may even try to pull themselves up from a sitting position.
- Your baby understands more and more of what you say. You may notice they respond when you say "no" or can find the ball when you say "Where's the ball?"
- You may hear your baby babble more and more. Communication improves and you may even hear "mama" and "dada". Of course, pointing, shaking their head and other gestures are also forms of communication you may notice.
- If it hasn't happened yet, your baby is probably beginning to show signs of separation anxiety. Your baby may not allow strangers or unfamiliar people to hold them so willingly anymore.

- **12 months old**

  - Get ready for cruising and walking! Your little one probably enjoys taking steps while holding onto chairs or another support. If they haven't started yet, your baby may also begin walking on their own quite soon.
  - Your baby may enjoy picking up small objects using their thumb, pointer and middle fingers. This is called the "pincer" grasp. Encourage the development of this grasp by providing small cooked vegetables and crackers or cereal to pick up.

o   Your baby's first tantrums may begin if they haven't already. Your baby's memory is getting stronger and they may remember what you've said "no" to. However, redirection is a great tactic to manage these outbursts. If you say no to a lollipop or grabbing a knife, offer something else to fulfill your baby's needs.

Materials

Once children reach the age of one, they have acquired many skills. They have grown from barely being able to sit on their own at about 6 months to walking or nearly walking at a year. Throughout this period, you can introduce a number of activities and materials that will encourage your child to grow and learn.

Similar to with your 0-6-month-old child, you should involve your baby in everyday life as much as possible. In fact, many of the materials and ideas mentioned here can be incorporated into your daily routines rather than using them out of context as a lesson.

As you continue to introduce new learning materials and activities to your child, follow your child's lead. One of the core principals of the Montessori philosophy is following the child. What does this mean exactly? Rather than the teachers and parents teaching the child what we think they need to know, we must observe the child's interests and abilities, and gently guide them towards materials and activities they will find interesting and meaningful. The child directs their own learning.

Many parents worry about whether their child gets enough tummy time, is crawling correctly or whether they are doing well for their age. It's understandable for parents to be concerned. After all, we want the best for our children. However, try to be patient with your child in their learning process.

When introducing materials and activities, don't dismay if your child isn't interested right away. Wait a few days or weeks and then try it again. Often, the second or third time your child will be ready to try it. Other times, your child will love an activity or material on the first try.

If your child seems particularly interested in a certain activity, look for other similar ways to practice the same skill. Or, look for ways to make the task slightly more challenging.

By following your child, you'll take full advantage of your child's interest and motivation to master a skill. With time, you'll become better and better at following your child and noticing what their needs are. Both you and your child will benefit from this important Montessori principal.

Another important point to mention as you enter into using more materials with your child is your role as guide and observer. Montessori believed in allowing children to work uninterrupted by adults. It is through this time of concentration that children learn to appreciate their success on their own.

It's possible for adults to avoid interruption in large part because Montessori materials and activities are self-correcting. This means that the child can easily discover if they've completed the activity correctly without relying on an adult for feedback. For example, if the child is putting lids on containers, there won't be any containers or lids left over once the activity is complete. Or, if not placed correctly, a puzzle piece won't fit.

Many new Montessori parents and teachers struggle to avoid intervening whether the intention is to help or praise the child. Try not to step in unless your child is showing true signs of frustration (crying and fussing) or is in danger of injuring themselves. By allowing your child to figure things out on their own, you're encouraging them to develop a love for the activity itself, an inner motivation not dependent on your praise. In addition, your child will concentrate longer and learn even more as they self-correct their own work.

Here are some suggested items to prepare or purchase for your 6-12-month-old baby:

Object Permanence Box

This box has a fancy name, but teaches a simple concept. Basically, it's a box with a hole in the top and an opening on the side, so that the child can put a ball in the hole and it falls down into the box and rolls out the other side. This teaches children that objects still exist even when they can't be seen. You can create your own version out of cardboard or wood, or buy one.

In addition to teaching object permanence, this material helps develop fine motor skills, and helps teach about cause and effect. Babies often begin enjoying this material around 8 months of age.

Wooden Push Toys

Because babies are just beginning to crawl, cruise and walk around this time, push toys are a great way to promote development of gross motor skills and their interest in these activities. Wooden push toys with wheels and good handles can be used to help your baby develop muscles and practice walking and pushing.

Anastasia told us that the "walker wagon" was her favorite amongst the toys for this age range. "All children at this age find great delight in pushing it around and putting blocks and other objects inside. It encourages children to make these first steps and provides additional support when learning to walk. I consider it a must-have for one year olds."

push wagon

Mirrors

In the same way when your baby was younger, provide low-hanging mirrors so that your baby can look at themself. Now that your baby is older, you may notice them making faces in the mirror, smiling or sticking out their tongue.

Imbucare Boxes

These boxes are similar to the object permanence boxes and got their name from the Italian word for *mail*. Imbucare boxes also have a hole on top to drop the ball in, but use a drawer underneath so that the child can pull out the drawer to find the ball.

Simple Puzzles w/ knobs

These should be 2 or 3 piece wooden puzzles with large knobs for the baby to grab. One typical Montessori puzzle features a square, circle and triangle.

Bells, whistles, drums, rattles, etc.

Your baby will enjoy hearing new sounds and making noise with these instruments. You can play listening games by playing the instruments from different areas of the house and waiting for your baby to find you. Whistles are particularly helpful for helping your baby exercise their mouth and direct their airflow.

Nesting Cups

These are great for both building a tower and putting the cups away. Your baby will start to be able to distinguish differences in size as well as develop fine motor skills.

Enjoying Time with Your Baby

Your baby continues to enjoy time with you immensely. A baby's parents are the most important beings in their life. Be sure to spend plenty of quality time with your baby, talking singing and playing together. Your strong connection and attachment will actually encourage your child's independence to develop because they feel secure in their relationship to you.

Now that your baby is older and becoming mobile, you can enjoy more activities together. In addition to reading, singing and the other activities you enjoy together, you can try some of these as well:

Making Sounds with Stories

This works especially well with books about animals. Preferably choose books that have actual photos of animals. As you page through, make sounds that animals make. Your baby will soon be good at imitating these sounds. Sounds for cars, trains, etc. are also great. Before you know it, your child will be able to recognize an image and make the sound associated with it.

> *Reading to the baby from the day he is born is the single best thing parents can do to assure baby's successful language development. One of the best pieces of advice I've been given is to continuously talk to the baby. I developed a habit of simply vocalizing my actions as I was doing something, for example, "Look, I am cutting this orange carrot to put in the delicious soup we are about to have for dinner". My baby always responds with a happy grin."*
>
> *-ANASTASIA*

Name the Parts of the Body

Language is an important part of your child's development. When focusing on teaching vocabulary, don't use other explanatory words, rather focus on the target words, in this case, the parts of the body. You can start with your nose, head, tummy and feet. Name them with your child regularly, and soon your child will be able to point to each body part you work on. This will soon help them be able to tell you if they're sick or if something hurts.

Imitating

Also, related to language development and communication, you can make faces and sounds and watch your baby copy you. Be silly! Stick out your tongue, cover your face with your hands and open your mouth wide.

Sorting Utensils

This is a practical life activity that you can enjoy with your baby. It's likely they're interested in eating and using utensils. Why not practice sorting between spoons and forks?

Provide your child with a basket of spoons and forks mixed together. Then, sort them, placing fork in one stack, and spoons in another.

Pouring Water

Water play is lots of fun for babies. Provide a space where your baby can get wet – you may even consider using the tub or sink! Just make sure you're close-by to help and supervise. Then, give your baby cups, bowls and pitchers to use for pouring. A ladle, slotted spoon and sieve can be fun as well. Then, let them enjoy the activity!

Using Lids

Start with one lid that can easily be placed on a container or box. Slowly, show your child how to remove the lid and put it back on.

Then, provide two containers or boxes and allow your child to experiment which lid goes on which container. You can increase the number gradually.

To add a further challenge to this activity, you can place objects such as large buttons or small balls inside each box or container.

Keep the material in a basket where your child can reach it.

Dropping Objects into Containers

Use objects such as pom poms, wooden sticks or very large buttons to place into a container. Show your child how to slowly place them in the container or jar. Then, allow your child to try. Experiment with different types of containers, moving from containers with wide openings to more narrow openings.

Collecting Nature Objects

Noticing objects in nature and picking them up is a wonderful sensory experience that allows your child to touch many different textures and encounter many colors and smells as well. Point out and pick up items such as pine cones, sticks, smooth stones, rough stones, shells, seeds, etc. Just ensure your baby doesn't put them in their mouth. You may even consider beginning a small nature table at your child's height. You can keep 2 or 3 objects on the table at a time from your walks and time outdoors.

Eating

Most parents begin feeding solids around 6 months of age. Consider using the principal of following your child when introducing new foods and feeding your child. One process that supports this idea is baby led weaning. Basically, this process allows parents to introduce foods that the whole family eats to their baby, only mashing or blending them so that they are safe for the baby to eat. Montessori supported this approach in her book The Montessori Method, where she suggested feeding babies polenta with tomatoes, olive oil and parmesan cheese as one of their first foods.

So, feel free to feed your baby whatever you're eating, as long as it won't pose a choking hazard. Eating should be an enjoyable time. Allow your baby to have a spoon as soon as possible to begin feeding themselves. It can be helpful to also hold a spoon yourself at first to help spoon feed your child. Your baby will also probably use their hands to eat, so make sure you help your baby wash them before offering food.

The Perfect Environment

Now that your little one is on the move, you can expect more exploration to happen. With this in mind, it's time to make sure your home is baby-friendly. Rather than looking at it as "baby proofing", consider the task's purpose to make the space safe and inviting for your baby.

Some important areas to consider are:

- Outlets
- Stairs
- Kitchen
- Bathroom

While you should ensure safety, this doesn't mean these areas should be cut off from your baby's reach. For stairs, you may want to consider using baby gates but also spending supervised time on the stairs so your baby can also have the freedom to explore and learn to climb.

Also, keep in mind that your baby will (if not already) be putting everything they can into their mouth. Avoid having very small or dangerous items within reach of your child. Some teething rings, cool washcloths to chew on and similar items will be helpful for your baby during this time.

In addition, based on the materials listed and what you find is most interesting for your baby, you should replace items on your baby's shelves so that they have access to the age-appropriate materials. You may consider introducing them one at a time so that your baby has time to adjust to each one.

You and Your Baby from 6-12 Months

Now, you know your baby much better! You are able to interact much more with your baby now that they actively imitate, babble and communicate with you. During this time, you will begin to notice your baby's character, likes and dislikes.

You'll quickly become accustomed to your baby on the move. You may experience a few bumps along the way, and it is so hard to watch your baby struggle, especially when they fall, but be strong! You are supporting your baby's independence. Although you'll want to step in and help, try to do so only when it's absolutely necessary. It's only through practice that your baby will learn and reach true independence.

The Next Steps

Mobility, curiosity and language will explode in the year from 1 to 2. You will watch as your baby transforms into a child, changing dramatically from the uncertain toddling 1-year-old. By 2 your child will be eating just about anything, have a mouth full of teeth, be able to run, jump and climb and communicate quite effectively.

Up until the age of 3, your child will continue to absorb and soak in everything they see in a way that is unlike any other stage in life. This means that you can harness this ability by using the activities suggested in this book and also allowing your child to participate fully in everyday life, especially multi-sensory experiences that involve many of the senses (touch, smell, taste, hearing and sight).

During this time your child will pick up even more on social norms and communication. Make sure you provide them with an excellent model by using manners with others and with your child. Even children as young as a year old may begin saying "Thank you" or "please" when they hear these words often.

Finally, your little one will begin to announce their independence as the world of talking opens up. You may hear "no" more often than you like. You'll also notice your child's determination to complete certain tasks all on their own, without your help. Independence grows from within your child and will flourish as they approach the age of 2,

So, get ready for the transition from baby to child! The journey is wonderful, exciting and full of adventure.

"The child who concentrates is immensely happy."
-MARIA MONTESSORI

CHAPTER FOUR

12-18 Months

From the time your baby turns 1, through 18 months is an exciting time. Your baby will likely begin walking during this time which is one of the most exciting advancements in independence for your baby.

As you look for milestones during this time, remember that many children walk or talk in their own time. As parents, we're so eager for them to develop these important skills that bring so much joy! However, each child knows their own time and will begin doing each when they are ready. Should you have concerns, you can always discuss it with your child's pediatrician.

Milestones

These milestones are much more generalized and can happen at any time between 12 and 18 months. Rather than marking out specific times when your child may reach these milestones, they will be listed with a description. As a parent, I know it can be stressful to compare your children to a milestone chart, especially at this age when things are even less predictable than in the first year of life. So, these milestones are listed not in any particular order, but can be expected to come along during this time period.

Growth Slows

The rapid growth associated with the first year of life slows at around 12 months. Your child will continue growing, but will also lose some of the baby fat as they become more and more mobile. All of that movement makes lean muscle.

Napping

Sleeping routines begin to change and many babies leave their morning nap behind.

Can Pretend

Your child may understand pretend play and enjoy "going to sleep" and "waking up."

Can Play Hide and Seek or Peekaboo Games

Your little one may begin to understand hiding and surprising others. Whether it's hiding under a cloth or blanket or hiding behind a wall, your little one will enjoy surprising you as well as being surprised.

Can Follow Instructions

Now that your baby understands much more, you may notice that your baby is able to follow simple instructions like "Bring me the cup" or "Go get a book."

Continues to Babble

Of course, your baby will continue to babble and talk as they explore their ability to communicate. You'll start to hear more imitations and your baby will start saying a few words if they haven't yet begun.

Can Drink from a Cup

If you haven't started giving your baby an open cup yet, now's a great time to start! Your baby can learn to use an open cup right away. This is great for your child's fine motor control, teeth and for learning consequences. At first, only put a small amount of liquid in the cup. Assist your child in holding the cup up to their mouth and tipping it so they can get a sip. Slowly, transfer the cup to your child's hands until they can do it on their own.

Can Use a Spoon

Now that your baby is eating solids, your child has probably become quite able at using a spoon. However, you can still expect your child to use a combination of the spoon and their hands while eating.

Can Walk

Around one year, most children are getting close to walking. Encourage your child to grab onto a low table or chair to "cruise" around. Soon enough your little one will be tottering around on their own!

Materials and Routines

Now that your child is mobile, they'll begin to have more control over which materials they choose to work with and also be able to participate in getting materials out and putting them away. Through this process, your child will begin to adopt many of the Montessori routines voluntarily without your intervention. In addition to materials, you'll also want to encourage these routines that you may have already begun with your younger child.

Routines

In a typical Montessori setting, children can choose where they work with materials. Children choose to work at a child-sized table or on the floor. When working on the floor, children use a carpet or rug. You can keep a rug or two in a handy location in your child's room, or wherever you're going to keep the materials. The rug helps the child define their workspace as they must keep all of the materials on the mat.

Encourage your child to keep all the materials on the carpet when working on the floor. Lead by example, and when working together, keep everything contained within this space.

When beginning working, you can ask your child to pick between a table and the floor to work. At first, you'll need to get out the carpet and show your child how to lay it out neatly, and then go get the material and place it on the mat. When finished, have your child help you roll or fold it up and put it away again.

As your child grows, you will notice they are more and more able to make choices regarding materials and work spaces. Try to help your child begin making these choices by allowing your child to pick a material. If it's hard for your child to choose, you can also offer two materials and see which one they seem to prefer.

Finally, each material must be returned to its place on the shelf when your child is finished working with it. Only one material should be out at a time. Help your child develop this sense of routine by cleaning up together until your child is able to do it on their own. When a carpet will no longer be used, roll it up and put it back in its place.

Materials

Educating the senses was one of Montessori's focuses for children ages 0-3. Why? The absorbent mind allows young children to intake extraordinary amounts of sensory related information. So, through the senses, children can create strong memories on which to draw later.

Montessori said:

"We cannot create observers by saying 'observe', but by giving them the power and the means for this observation and these means are procured through education of the senses."

So, when choosing materials and activities, try to include as many of the senses as possible.

Now, you can also begin giving slightly more formal "presentations" of the materials you use. A presentation is a lesson or demonstration of how the material works and what is to be done in the activity. Some materials are more free-flowing and won't require a formal presentation.

Start by smiling at your child to ensure that you have their full attention. Then, show your child the material you're going to use and set it up. Connect with a smile again. Then, slowly demonstrate what your child needs to do. Use slow movements and don't talk about what you're doing. Let your actions do the teaching unless words are required in the presentation. Following your demonstration, allow your child to work alone with the material for as long as they desire and are using the material correctly.

Children are curious, and will often find an incorrect way to use a material. For example, your child may throw blocks. Remind your child how to use the material. If your child continues in this manner, explain to your child that you will have to put the blocks away. Help your child put them away if necessary. Later, also offer your child an alternative that fulfills the need expressed, which in this case could be a throwing the ball into the basket game. If the same behavior continues with the blocks, you may remove them from the shelf for a time until your child is ready to use them correctly again.

Wooden Blocks

At this age, children can begin to build and knock down towers. The open-ended possibilities with wooden blocks offer a chance for the child to explore. Fine motor control is developed and your child will also learn about causes and consequences.

Cloth/Soft Balls

Improve hand-eye coordination and enjoy some fun by rolling or tossing a soft ball back and forth. Learning to throw a ball is a job all in itself! You may also want to use a large basket and practice throwing the ball in it as well.

Sensory Bins

While not a traditional Montessori material this concept plays into the idea of developing the senses well. With sensory bins, you can introduce your child to may new textures and natural objects in an open-ended play opportunity. Just be sure that you supervise so that your child doesn't endanger themselves by putting items in their mouth. Some popular options may include:

- Water theme with sieves, measuring cups, funnels, bowls, etc.
- Sand theme with similar items to water theme.
- Seasonal theme with natural objects from outside (a winter theme may include pinecones, pine needles, cotton balls for "snow", etc.)

Infant Dressing Frames

The infant dressing frames help children begin practicing skills used to help them dress and undress. Some of the best first dressing frames include Velcro, large buttons, snaps and zippers. These frames typically feature only 3 pieces to connect rather than 5 or more at the primary (3-6-year-old) level. Demonstrate this material with a presentation. Introduce only one frame at a time and only one in a day. Once all have been presented, you may leave them all out on the shelf.

Clothespins

Provide your child with a basket with clothespins placed around the edge. Show your child how you take each pin off and then put the back on. For a while, your child may only succeed in removing the pins, but eventually they'll gain the necessary strength to replace them as well.

"Piggy Bank"

Similar to the object permanence boxes, a piggy bank material uses the same concept, but uses coins or buttons instead of the ball. You can make one on your own with an old yogurt tub. First, cover or paint the container to avoid distractions. Then cut a slit in the lid, where your child will insert the coins or buttons. Place both the piggy bank and a basket with the buttons or coins on a tray. Demonstrate the activity first, and then allow your child to try

Using Cookie Cutters with Bread

Cookie cutters are a great way to practice fine motor skills, sharing and to develop snack preparations skills. Provide your child with a slice of bread and show them how to use the cookie cutter to cut out a shape. This also works well with thinly sliced watermelon and cantaloupe. Demonstrate this activity first.

Slicing Bananas

Your child can also practice slicing bananas and other soft foods. This helps them improve their mealtime skills and fine motor skills. It's also a great way to enjoy snack time even more than usual. Special slicers can be purchased, which are held at the top, rather than a bread knife which requires a bit more coordination. Show your child how to carefully peel the banana and demonstrate how to slice.

Set up a tray with the fruit, knife or slicer, a cutting board and a plate for placing the slices. You can do this activity in your kitchen, or add it onto a shelf for your child to access.

Enjoying Time with Your Child

Life just gets more and more exciting as your child grows. You are able to watch them master many new skills and experience new things. In an effort to involve your child in your everyday life, be sure to include them in the practical routines outlined below.

Your child will enjoy imitating you in everyday chores as well as swell with pride in their ability to contribute. Independence is also fostered through their participation in these tasks. Here are some easy ways to enjoy time with your child in practical ways:

Sweeping

Purchase a child-sized broom for your child to use while you sweep with an adult-sized broom.

In addition to sweeping together, you may also consider setting up a practical life activity for your child. For this activity, you'll need a small dust pan and brush for your child to use. You can use pieces of cut up paper or pom poms in a basket to practice with. Show your child how to dump out the items in the basket either onto a table or the floor. Then demonstrate how to use the dust pan and brush. Allow your child to try.

Washing Dishes

With a proper stool and supervision, you can allow your child to help wash dishes at the sink. Alternatively, use two wash basins on a low table so that your child may practice this skill. You can demonstrate the process, providing your child with only 2 or 3 dishes at a time to work on while they get the hang of it.

Art Projects

Your child can enjoy more and more art projects as they grow. Coloring, painting, playing with play dough, ripping paper and using glue are just a few of the activities you can get started with. As you embark on your art project adventures, remember to use routines with your child that they can get used to and follow later. Some routines and habits you may want to use include: using a smock, laying out a sheet of newspaper on the table before painting, helping wash up when done, etc.

Setting the Table

When it's mealtime, have your little one help set their small table up. Demonstrate how to arrange the pate, eating utensils, napkin and cup on the table. Then allow your child to do it.

Going for a Walk

Little ones love to go for walks. Adults can also enjoy this as an activity, but we are often so focused on getting somewhere, we are unable to enjoy the journey. Try to enjoy the act of walking.

You may also try doing a "theme" walk where you look for a certain color, or count birds or cars, depending on the interest of your little one. A collecting walk where you collect nature items such as stones or leaves can also be fun.

Montessori sums up walking in a lovely way:

"The child of two is well able to walk for a mile or two. The difficult parts of the walk appeal to him the most. The child is not trying to "get there." All he wants is to walk. And because his legs are shorter than ours, we must not try to make him keep up with us.

The child does not walk only with his legs, he also walks with his eyes. Sees a flower-smells it-sees a tree-goes up to it. If some obstacle lies across his path, for example some fallen rocks or a tree trunk, then his happiness is complete."

Provide opportunities for walks like this, with no other objective beyond enjoying and exploring what surrounds you.

Self-Care

You can begin teaching your child to complete basic hygiene activities on their own. For example, brushing teeth, washing hands, washing the face and combing hair are all activities your child can complete with supervision. Slowly demonstrate each activity and invite your child to try.

As you can see, most of the above activities fall into the "practical life" category in which useful life skills are taught. There are many more ways to involve your child in practical life skills. Whenever possible, involve your child in daily chores, cleaning, cooking and washing. They are sure to enjoy it and gain so much from participating.

"I love making butter with young toddlers. Simply pour milk in a glass jar and place a clean marble inside, screw the lid tightly and give it to your child

> to shake. It will take some time, but eventually milk will turn into fluffy butter,
> it's easy and mess free. Later child can enjoy handmade butter spreading it on
> a toast."

> -ANASTASIA

The Perfect Environment

As your child grows and continues to explore, you'll need to make sure your home is set-up so that your child can access all of the things they need to access. This is to encourage your child to continue on their journey towards independence. Some considerations include:

Sink Access

Use a step stool so that your child can reach the sink properly to wash hands. You may still supervise your child, but it's important that they can begin performing this task on their own.

Water Access

If you feel your child is ready, you may consider keeping some cups in a low cupboard so that your child may access them for drinking water. You may use a cooler or similar water holding device with a spigot so that your toddler can get water when they need it. It may take a few days of guidance for your child to become accustomed to the idea and use the water only for drinking, rather than play.

Cleaning Supplies

With growing independence come accidents. Keep some rags, a child-sized broom, dust pan, bucket, sponge and similar items in an easily accessible place. Show your child how to use each item and where it's kept. This way your child can feel in control when accidents happen.

"Through practical exercises of this sort the children develop a true 'social feeling', for they are working in the environment of the community in which they live, without concerning themselves as to whether it is for their own, or for the common good."
-MARIA MONTESSORI

CHAPTER FIVE

18-24 Months

Your little baby is now looking and acting more and more like a child. By this point, your little one is probably quite stable on their feet and quickly improving both fine and gross motor skills. You probably feel amazed at how far your little one has come.

Routines are now much more of a habit for your little one. So, if you regularly leave your child at a daycare center or with a family member, separation anxiety has probably lessened, or will soon.

Over the coming months, your child will make leaps and bounds in their language development, learning up to a few new words each day. With these advances in communication, your child will make their wants and needs even more clearly and may begin to delight in saying "no!" with gusto.

Milestones

Below is a list of some of the milestones and skills you can expect your child to master over the coming months. Some of these can also help direct the activities you do together. As you notice your child showing interest in one of these skills, try to provide as much opportunity to work on it as possible.

Montessori called times of motivation and interest in mastering a specific skill "sensitive periods." It is during these times that your child may show repetitive behaviors and insistence, as if driven by an inner force, to complete a certain activity. For example, your child may insist on singing a song over and over again. Or, your child may insist on opening a container on their own. Or perhaps your child will stubbornly climb up and down the steps dozens of times in the same day. Encourage your child during these sensitive periods. Their motivation, concentration and interest will allow for great advancement.

Reads

Your child may now "read" to themselves, using a sing song voice or babbling while looking at their favorite books. Encourage this helpful practice by making books available for them to use on a low shelf. Also, make sure to take time to read together every day. Remember, at this age your child will enjoy repetition. Each time they hear the book, they learn something new and enjoy it more and more as they know what to expect.

May Speak in Phrases

Rather than saying only one word at a time, your child will begin to say 2 or 3 words together. For example, "no ball" or "me happy." At this point your child may still mix up "I, you, me" and other pronouns, but eventually they'll sort them out. Encourage all of the effort your child is making. At this point, there's no need to correct. If you'd like, you can simply repeat the phrase correctly or answer them, for example "I'm happy!" or "You're happy!" after they say "me happy."

Can Undress

You may be surprised to find a pantsless or diaperless child running around. As your child's motor skills continue to improve, they will quickly learn to remove clothes and enjoy running around nude. You can certainly allow your child the freedom to run around with no clothes on, or you can calmly explain that we wear clothes to keep from getting cold and when we go outside. Helping your child learn how to put clothes on is also a great strategy for encouraging interest in dressing as well as undressing.

Climbs

Stairs and the challenge of climbing up onto chairs and other furniture is probably very attractive for your little one. Give your little one plenty of opportunities to practice in a supervised way. Trips to the park where there are climbing structures are a great place to start.

Identifies Objects and People in Pictures

Now when you're reading books together, you may be able to ask your child to point to different items, animals or people. Photo albums also become interesting for pointing out mama, papa, siblings and other family members.

Notices Wrong Words

In a similar way that your child identifies images in a book, they'll also notice if you call a dog a cow. If you ask "Is this a cow?" they may shake their head "no" or even say "no!"

Sings Songs

If your little one hasn't started humming along yet, they may begin now. You're little one may sing the words or just "lalala." Take advantage of singing songs to teach hand motions too.

May Jump

Your child may show interest in jumping using both legs simultaneously to hop. This will soon grow into trying to hop down and even up stairs. Practice with them for fun!

R MCKINNEY

Interest in Potty Learning

Around this age some children begin to show interest in potty learning. Behaviors such as following you to the bathroom, staying dry during a nap, the ability to pull pants down and an interest in underwear are just some of the signs you may notice. Just like any other Montessori lesson, you'll need to follow your child's lead for successful potty learning.

More Pronounced Tantrums

Most parents dread experiencing tantrums. However, they are a normal part of toddlerhood. Some children may begin earlier than 18 months and some children have tantrums right up through the preschool years.

Because young children can't communicate what they feel or want, this great frustration is often communicated through a tantrum. Children express anger, fear, frustration and sadness through upsets. While these strong shows of feeling can be uncomfortable, stressful and unpleasant for us grownups, they are a rite of passage for little ones.

To weather these upsets, consider some of these helpful techniques:

- Help your child identify their feelings. You can do this by saying "You seem angry," or "I can tell you're frustrated."
- Without breaking your rules or guidelines, stay present for your child. By crying and screaming, your child is releasing tension. However, if your child is upset because you won't let them have or do something, stick to your word. You can stay close to your child and say "I'll be ready to give you a hug whenever you want."
- After the upset, find a way to meet needs. If your child is hungry and wanted candy, provide healthy food. Or, if your child wanted to do something that's too dangerous such as climb on top of the couch, give your child the opportunity to climb at the playground as soon as possible.
- Reconnect with your child as soon as possible. As soon as your child is ready, hug or comfort them. You may want to take some time to have a laugh or read a book together to reinforce your positive connection. Sometimes children

have upsets because they need more time with you. In these cases, a time to reconnect is just what your child is craving.

Materials

Now your child's brain and motor skills have developed further, preparing them for more complicated activities, and greater use of language. Whereas before, demonstrations usually involve very few words, now, the focus on some lessons may actually be vocabulary.

In addition to the materials listed below, your child will likely want to continue practicing with familiar materials. Add a new layer of difficulty to the materials your child already knows. For example, provide a puzzle with more than 3 pieces. Or, string up a clothesline to use with the clothespins. Continue to provide opportunities to cut and slice foods. Wherever possible, follow your child's lead and see where it takes you!

Color Matching

For this activity, use simple objects without another function. Start with the primary colors: blue, red and yellow. Put 2 items of each color in a basket. The items could be buttons, colored paper pasted to a small block of wood or something similar. To demonstrate the activity, lay all of the items out on a mat or table. Put three of the items in a vertical row. Then select another item and compare it to each of the other three. Find the match and place it beside the match. Continue until each color has its match. Then, invite your child to try.

Saying Colors, Body Parts, Other Vocabulary

For this activity, ask your child to repeat after you. Pick 3-6 words to use. Say them together while pointing at the objects. Then, ask your child to point to each object you say. Finally ask your child "what is this?" while pointing to the object. This is known as the 3-period-lesson, as there are 3 stages (repeating, pointing and saying).

Matching Shapes

In a similar manner to "matching colors" use either wooden shapes or sturdy paper cut outs to teach 3 shapes. Good ones to start with are a triangle, square and circle. You'll need pairs of each shape, 6 items total (3 pairs).

Smelling Jars

You can purchase or create your very own smelling jars. Three jars is a good number to start with. Consider washing and reusing old spice jars. Use strong smells such as mint, cinnamon, banana, etc. Then, show your child how to smell each jar.

Grouping Items

Similar to matching items, grouping items requires the child to discern between categories. However, in this activity, more objects are used. Start with only two categories. For example, place about 10 popsicle sticks and 10 marbles in a basket. Show your child how to remove each item and place it on the mat. Make a vertical column of sticks and one of marbles. Allow your child to try grouping. You can easily make this activity more difficult by including 3 items or more as your child becomes better and better. Items found in nature make great choices for this activity. Pinecones, acorns, sticks, leaves, etc. add a wonderful sensory experience.

Spooning

For this material, you need to beautiful bowls, a spoon, dry beans and a tray. Place all of the beans in one bowl on the left side of the tray. The empty bowl should be on the right side and the spoon horizontally below the bowls. Show your child how to use the spoon to carefully spoon the beans from the bowl on the left to the one on the right. If any beans spill onto the tray, carefully pick them up with your fingers and place them in the bowl on the right. Allow your child to try.

As your child enjoys this activity, you may add variety by exchanging the beans for rice or other grains and switching bowls as well. A variety of spoons can also be enjoyed, from small spoons to soup spoons to ladles.

Pouring

This material is similar to spooning, but requires a small pitcher and a cup rather than the two bowls and a spoon. Use grains as well to begin and then move towards smaller grains and finally water as your child's skill improves. As your child advances, consider adding another cup, changing pitcher size, etc. to keep the activity challenging.

Enjoying Time with Your Child

As your child's independence continues to increase, you can give them more responsibilities. This will encourage your child on their journey of learning and help them build their character.

Although young children still have a difficult time understanding many social norms, you can also begin to teach them lessons in grace and courtesy. From the basics of being polite to how to share, these are lessons that will serve them a lifetime. At this point, most of what you do should be through example. However, you can also encourage their social and emotional growth with a few activities.

Sharing

There are many ways to encourage sharing, the first of which is by example. Another great activity to teach is sharing a snack. Ideally you can do this with a small group of children. Prepare a healthy snack such as apple slices or popcorn. Invite the children to pass the bowl or plate around the table and to each take a slice or small bowlful of popcorn. Each child should say "thank you" to the one who passed it to them. The other should say "your welcome." Allow the children to enjoy the snack together.

In toddler and preschool classrooms, when children complete slicing exercises, they may also be provided with toothpicks. The child can place the slice of food (banana, cucumber, cheese, etc.) on a plate and place a toothpick in each piece. Then, the child carries the plate around the room and offers the snack to others. Your child can do this in your home with family members or friends.

More Advanced Self Care

You can teach your child more advanced lessons in self-care such as blowing the nose, applying lotion, washing their own hair at bath time, etc.

Potty learning, as mentioned earlier is also often an interest at this age. If your child seems interested, use the Montessori approach of following your child to work on potty learning. Remember this is a skill your child will master, not one that you will teach or force. The more initiative your child shows, the more successful it will be. So, following their lead, take it slow and help guide them through the process.

For potty learning, you'll need some materials:
- A small training potty
- A stool to help get on the big potty
- Underwear (accessible to your child)
- Rags to clean up after accidents
- A hamper for wet clothes

When starting potty learning, you may consider putting the small training potty in the bathroom or even in your child's room so that they can grow accustomed to it.

For potty learning to begin, you'll need to demonstrate using the potty. If you don't usually allow your child to follow you into the bathroom, consider allowing this so that your child can see exactly how to use the bathroom. Then, show your child the small potty and explain what it's for.

Show your child the underwear and explain that you're going to use underwear instead of a diaper. For the first few days, you may even consider allowing your child to be bottomless in the home so that they don't struggle with clothing when using the potty. Then, be sure to use cloth underwear so that your child can feel when they have an accident, experiencing the sensation and noticing the outcome.

At first, accidents are to be expected. Treat these in a matter of fact manner. Ask your child to help you clean up and change clothes. In order to reduce the number of accidents, ask your child if they need to use the potty throughout the day. This will help your child remember to think about the sensations they feel in their body and notice whether or not they need to use the bathroom.

At night, you may still need to use diapers for a while. Children have a hard time getting used to waking up in the night to go to the bathroom. Even children as old as 4 or 5 may still need diapers at night. However, in their own time, your child will indeed learn to get up and go to the potty.

Potty learning is a process. Be positive and encouraging of your child's efforts. If it seems too frustrating, you may want to return to diapers and try again once your child is a bit older.

Art Projects

Most young children continue to enjoy arts and crafts as they grow. At this stage, you may consider providing some basic art supplies such as blank paper and crayons so that your child has access to them whenever they please. As your child grows more and more capable, consider providing additional materials such as scissors, play dough, paint, etc. so that they can use these whenever they like.

More Advanced Practical Life

Continue to involve your child in everyday chores such as sweeping, washing dishes and setting the table. Some other great practical life chores for your little one include:

- Watering plants (houseplants and in the garden)
- Wiping down the table
- Dusting furniture
- Washing clothes by hand
- Washing shoes with water and a brush

- Helping with cooking and baking

Just about any chore around the home can incorporate the help of a young child. It is through these activities that your child grows in independence and confidence. Watch as they purposefully participate in the home and develop a sense of responsibility that will only grow in years to come.

The Perfect Environment

By now you've probably made your home very child-friendly in a Montessori way. Every so often, it's important for you to re-evaluate your child's environment and how it's being used. For example, are there materials your child is no longer interested in on the shelf? Do you now need to provide a greater selection of books for your child to choose from? What needs does your child have for workspace? Perhaps the table you started out with is now too small for laying out larger projects.

In order to help you re-evaluate, take a walk through your home, imagining that you are your child. Notice at what height the things you need to access are located. Is anything too low or too high? Perhaps you need more stools, or stools of a different size. Do you have a nice spot to sit and read books and a space to move and jump around? Also, observe your child's routines and movements.

Then, double check to make sure everything is orderly and neat. Your child craves an orderly environment where it's clear that everything has a place. Also, ensure that while an array of activities is provided, you aren't overwhelming your child. Avoid introducing many new materials at once, rather change them one or two at a time, leaving a few days in between each addition.

Now that your little one will likely be more and more involved in dressing themselves, place a hamper in your child's room if you haven't done so yet. Also, adjust any drawers, shelves and closet space so that your child can easily reach all of their clothes.

Once your observations are complete, make any changes you feel are necessary to your space. Constant evaluation is required to maintain the ideal environment in your home for both you and your child. Experiment and adjust as necessary as your child continues to grow.

> *"Remove electronic toys, turn off the TV and iPad, invite your toddler to join you preparing a meal, allow them to move freely with minimum restriction for movement and discovery when safe to do so."*
>
> *-ANASTASIA*

You and Your Child from 0-2 Years

You've made it! The journey from 0-2 years is a long and short one. Some days (and nights) may have felt unending, but by the time your little one turns 2, you'll be wondering where all the time went!

The journey from birth through the age of two is a story of connection, mastering independence and sensory exploration. Your relationship to your child is the most important part of the journey, as it is through your connection with your child that you will help guide them through their journey to independence and sensory exploration.

Treasure each moment along the way, and remember that during the most difficult moments that you can make it through. Children are only small once, and it's amazing to watch them grow.

Resources

Caldwell, Dr. Bettye. "Developmental Checklist: 12-18 Months". *Fisher-price.com*. N.p., 2016. Web. 21 Nov. 2016.

Chitwood, Deb. "How To Prepare A Montessori Baby Room". *Living Montessori Now*. N.p., 2016. Web. 21 Nov. 2016.

"How We Montessori". *how we montessori*. N.p., 2016. Web. 21 Nov. 2016.

Irinyi, Michelle and Michelle Irinyi. "Conscious Interaction With Infants – Supporting Global Childhood Development". *Montessoritraining.blogspot.ca*. N.p., 2016. Web. 21 Nov. 2016.

Irinyi, Michelle and Michelle Irinyi. "The Absorbent Mind, Chapter 9: The First Days Of Life". *Montessoritraining.blogspot.ca*. N.p., 2016. Web. 21 Nov. 2016.

Irinyi, Michelle. "Developing Object Permanence Skills In The Montessori Environment". *Montessoritraining.blogspot.com*. N.p., 2016. Web. 21 Nov. 2016.

Irinyi, Michelle. "Introducing Foods By Following The Child - A Montessori Approach". *Montessoritraining.blogspot.com*. N.p., 2016. Web. 21 Nov. 2016.

Irinyi, Michelle. "Traditional Montessori Materials In The Infant/Toddler Environment". *Montessoritraining.blogspot.com*. N.p., 2016. Web. 21 Nov. 2016.

Irinyi, Michelle. "Traditional Montessori Materials In The Infant/Toddler Environment". *Montessoritraining.blogspot.com*. N.p., 2016. Web. 21 Nov. 2016.

"Let's Start At The Very Beginning: Montessori For Infants - Montessori For Everyone - Montessori Blog". *Montessori for Everyone - Montessori Blog*. N.p., 2016. Web. 21 Nov. 2016.

"Milestones For An 18-Month-Old Child-Topic Overview". *WebMD*. N.p., 2016. Web. 21 Nov. 2016.

"Montessori Infant Mobiles - A Summary And My Recommendations". *how we montessori*. N.p., 2016. Web. 21 Nov. 2016.

Pregnancy Birth and Baby. *Pregnancybirthbaby.org.au*. N.p., 2016. Web. 21 Nov. 2016.

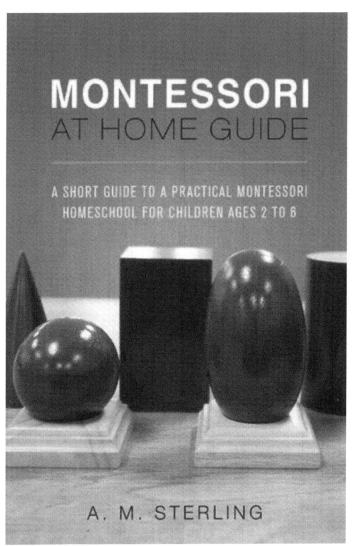

MONTESSORI
AT HOME GUIDE

A SHORT GUIDE TO A PRACTICAL MONTESSORI
HOMESCHOOL FOR CHILDREN AGES 2 TO 6

A. M. STERLING

Other books in the "Montessori at Home Guide" series include.

MONTESSORI
AT HOME GUIDE

101 MONTESSORI INSPIRED *ACTIVITIES*
FOR CHILDREN AGES 2-6

A. M. STERLING

MONTESSORI
AT HOME GUIDE

A SHORT PRACTICAL MODEL TO GENTLY GUIDE
YOUR *2-6* YEAR OLD THROUGH LEARNING
Self-Care

RACHEL PEACHEY

Sign up to receive email updates on new releases at:
http://www.sterlingproduction.com

About the Authors

Ashley and Mitch Sterling are author/indie-publishers and video-bloggers on YouTube known as 'Fly by Family'. When they're not writing or talking to a camera lens, the Sterlings value their time together, in the beautiful bluegrass-laden wilderness of eastern Kentucky, where they live with their two children, Nova and Mars.

Their company, Sterling Production, specializes in producing easy to read guides to help parents get a jump-start on incorporating Montessori inspired learning in their home. These books are created with the busy parent in mind, simplifying their experience with guides that are short and to the point.

Visit our website: www.sterlingproduction.com
Visit our YouTube: www.youtube.com/flybyfamily

Thank you for reading our book! We would love to hear from you in an honest review on Amazon or Goodreads!
Sincerely,
Ashley and Mitchell Sterling

Made in the USA
San Bernardino, CA
18 May 2019